# TEMPLE GRANDIN, Ph.D.

# The Way I See It

**REVISED & EXPANDED**
**2nd EDITION**
*with 14 New Articles*

*A Personal Look at Autism & Asperger's*

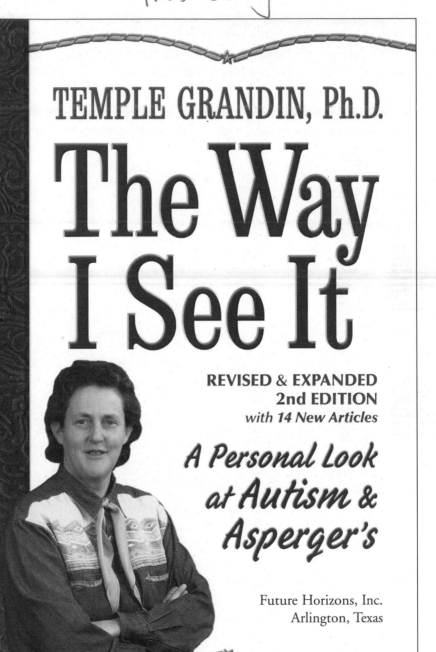

Future Horizons, Inc.
Arlington, Texas

721 W. Abram Street
Arlington, TX 76013
Toll-free: 800.489.0727
Phone: 817.277.0727
Fax: 817.277.2270
Website: *www.FHautism.com*
E-mail: *info@FHautism.com*

Second Edition

Printed in Canada

Cover and interior design © TLC Graphics, *www.TLCGraphics.com*
Cover: Monica Thomas; Interior: Erin Stark

Cover photo © Rosalie Winard
Photos on pages 25, 79, 233, and 263 © Rosalie Winard
*www.rosaliewinard.com*

Publisher's Cataloging-In-Publication Data
(Prepared by The Donohue Group, Inc.)
Grandin, Temple.
   The way I see it : a personal look at autism & Asperger's / Temple Grandin. — Rev. and exp. 2nd ed.

   p. : ill. ;  cm.

   "Revised & expanded 2nd ed. with 13 new articles."
   Includes bibliographical references and index.
   ISBN: 978-1-935274-21-6

   1. Autism—Popular works.  2. Asperger's syndrome—Popular works.  3. Autism in children.  4. Asperger's syndrome in children.  5. Autistic people—Life skills guides.  I. Title.
RC553.A88 G743 2011
616.85882

# Also by Temple Grandin

*I dedicate this book to all individuals
on the autism spectrum.*

# Acknowledgments

I WOULD LIKE TO ACKNOWLEDGE VERONICA ZYSK, MY EDITOR AT Future Horizons, who edited both my articles in the *Autism Asperger's Digest* magazine, and this book. Without her hard work and guidance, this book would not have been possible.

# Contents

pany, I realized it was possible for me to lead that charge and produce a film about her extraordinary life. I called Temple, reached out to HBO, and we were on our way. It took us ten years to get it right, but I couldn't be more proud of our film, *Temple Grandin*, which celebrates the life of someone I respect and admire so much. Whether I was sharing a meal with her in New York, reviewing dailies with her in my hotel room in Austin, sitting beside her at the Golden Globes, being hugged by her on stage at the Emmys, or listening to her encourage the Chairman of Time Warner to examine the McDonald's distribution system, my days with Temple have been amongst the best and most interesting of my life.

After settling back into my normal life, I picked up a copy of Temple's book *The Way I See It*. Just when I thought I had learned everything Temple could teach me, I was astonished to learn there was more—a lot more. Often parents of children with autism are encouraged to adhere to a routine with their child. Temple devotes an entire chapter to encouraging flexibility in a routine and provides examples on how to accomplish that. She identifies strategies for encouraging interests that can later become vocations, as children with autism become adults with autism. Additionally, Temple reminds us that learning is a continuum. Human beings have the ability to learn well into their senior years, and the exposure to new things is essential in expanding a person's mind, even, and perhaps especially, if they have autism. This book is insightful, helpful, and hopeful—just like the woman who wrote it! It is a "how-to" guide that I am confident will leave any reader feeling both informed and inspired.

EMILY GERSON SAINES
February 2011

# Foreword to First Edition
## by Dr. Ruth Sullivan

WHO BETTER THAN TEMPLE GRANDIN TO GIVE US A PERSONAL look at autism and Asperger's?

For over thirty of her nearly sixty years' experience on the autism spectrum, Temple has dedicated much of her time, energy, considerable intellect, and talents to learning about her condition and translating it for the rest of us. This book puts together under one cover her highly insightful, informed, articulate, and most of all, practical, ideas and instructions for dealing with the wide range of behaviors, learning styles, and physical health issues found in autism and Asperger's Syndrome.

At the time Temple came on the autism scene, few people had heard of autism, and even fewer had ever heard of someone with autism who could communicate well enough to tell us how it felt, from the inside. I was a member of a small group of parents of children with autism, nationwide, who in November 1965, at the invitation of Dr. Bernard Rimland, met to form a national organization, the National Society for Autistic Children (NSAC), now called the Autism Society of America (ASA). Our goal was to seek a better understanding of this mysterious condition that so severely affected our children, and to seek treatment, as well as cause and cure. There was almost nothing in the literature. Dr. Rimland's book, *Infantile Autism: The Syndrome and Its Implications for a Neural Theory of Behavior* (published in 1964) was among the very first on the subject. None of us knew an adult with autism.

I first met Temple in the mid-1980s at the St. Louis Airport, when making a connection to Chicago for the annual NSAC conference. In the small waiting area there were about 25 other conference goers from across the nation, also waiting for that flight. Most of us knew each other, and the talk was mostly about autism.

Standing on the periphery of the group was a tall young woman who was obviously interested in the discussions. She seemed shy and pleasant, but mostly she just listened. Once in Chicago, she and I got on the conference bus and sat together as we traveled to our hotel. I learned her name was Temple Grandin, and this was her first autism conference. I was impressed at how much she knew about the condition. It wasn't until later in the week that I realized she was someone with autism. I had heard of a woman who had that diagnosis, who was high-functioning, but had not connected the two. I approached her and asked if she'd be willing to speak at the next year's NSAC conference program. She agreed.

Back then, NSAC conferences were the only national meetings focused solely on autism. Each year there was one entire session set aside just for information exchange. It was held in a large room of ten-person round tables, each designated for a special subject, with a discussion leader. That next year I was the discussion leader for a table labeled "Adults with Autism," and that's where Temple first addressed an NSAC audience. The ten chairs were filled immediately, and people were standing at least three deep. The room became noisy, and with so many wanting to hear every word Temple said, I asked for a room just for us. More people followed as we were led to a small auditorium.

Temple and I stood on the slightly elevated stage. The audience couldn't get enough of her. Here, for the first time, was someone who could tell us from her own experience what it was like to be extremely sound sensitive ("like being tied to the rail and the train's coming"). On the topic of wearing certain kinds of underwear, she described her profound skin sensitivity, and how she could not verbally articulate how painful it was. On relationships, she talked about how hard it was to communicate what she felt, and about her difficulty in understanding others. She was asked many questions: "Why does my son do so much spinning?" "What can I do about toilet training?" "Why does he hold his hands to his ears?" "Why doesn't he look at me?" She spoke from her own experience, and her insight was impressive. There were tears in more than one set of eyes that day.

After the hour-long session ended, many stayed around to talk to Temple. She seemed surprised but pleased with the attention—even adulation. Later, when I asked, she said she had been a little nervous. Over the years, I've often thought about that scene, and marveled at how remarkable an event it was for her, and all of us.

Not long afterwards, in 1986, her first book was published, *Emergence: Labeled Autistic.* The rest is history, as they say. Ten years later came her highly acclaimed work, *Thinking in Pictures,* with other autism books to follow. Temple simultaneously became well known for her work and writings in her chosen professional field of animal behavior. She earned a Ph.D. in that discipline, from the University of Colorado. Her 2006 release, *Animals in Translation,* became a *New York Times* Bestseller.

Temple quickly became a much sought-after speaker in the autism community. She wrote articles for the popular press as well as peer-reviewed professional journals. Always generous to projects related to parents and their children, she wrote for parent organization newsletters, and traveled around the U.S. and the world to speak at autism conferences. Probably no one with autism has appeared in the world media more than Temple, nor had a bigger impact on our global understanding of autism and Asperger's Syndrome and the people diagnosed on the spectrum.

Yet, the Temple Grandin of today is not the same woman I met nearly twenty-five years ago. It has been a remarkable privilege to witness Temple's growth in social skills and awareness throughout the time I have known her. She is one of the hardest workers I have ever known. In my opinion, it is mainly that trait that has helped her become the successful, engaging adult she is now, despite severe difficulties along the way. She is knowledgeable. She is willing to help parents as well as others with autism. She is insightful. And she is courageous—a fitting word to explain her heartfelt, strong (and sometimes unwanted) advice to her adult peers with autism or Asperger's on the importance of being polite, dressing appropriately, accepting responsibility for their actions and following rules of civility if they want to get and keep a job or have friends.

And not least, she is funny. Though generally her presentations are straightforward, in recent years she has become quite good at humor. Her audiences love it.

In addition, and to her credit, she has learned to be generous in recognizing those who have helped her along the way, namely her mother, Eustacia Cutler, whose book, *A Thorn in My Pocket*, tells the family story. Others are teachers and colleagues who saw her potential and bravely went beyond current practice to help her develop some of her strengths. For many individuals with autism, it is difficult-to-impossible to understand and develop "theory of mind," that intangible mental process by which most of us intuitively notice and "read" the nuances of social situations: how others are feeling, what they may be thinking, and the meaning behind their nonverbal actions. Temple's persistence in learning this, and her strong analytical skills while doing so, have helped significantly in improving her social thinking and social sense.

Temple continues to wrap her energies around autism and the people it touches. Her talent is a gift to all of us—not just those of us in the autism community, but the world at large. The book you are holding in your hand is the result of her keen detective-like analysis of human beings, her extensive personal thought, and the wisdom gained only through the personal experiences that make up Temple Grandin. It serves as an excellent summary of what one human being has contributed to one of the most disabling and puzzling conditions known to mankind. Temple takes time to listen—without pre-conceived ideas or judgment—to parents and the professionals who work with and for individuals with autism on the entire spectrum, from severe autism to high-level Asperger's. She seeks *solutions*, from teaching strategies to the larger lifespan issues that can present challenges of immense proportions, even for neurotypicals. The suggestions she offers in this book are imaginative, well thought out, practical, and useful. She talks directly to the reader, with honesty and understanding. She knows what autism is like, and her recommendations make sense.

Every library, large or small, needs this book on its shelves. Every school, large or small, with the responsibility of educating children with autism or Asperger's, needs the guidance this book offers. Every teacher within those schools will benefit from reading it and applying the strategies Temple so clearly illuminates. Last, and certainly not least, every parent will find within these pages golden nuggets of advice, encouragement, and hope to fuel their day-to-day journey through their child's autism.

As I've heard Temple often remark in the twenty-something years I have known her, about the way she views autism and her life: "I didn't become social overnight. There wasn't a point when some magic switch turned on in my brain and the social stuff made sense after that. I'm the person I am today because of all the experiences I've had, and the opportunities those experiences offered me to learn, little by little. It wasn't easy; sometimes it was really difficult. I've made a lot of mistakes, but I just kept going until I got it right. And, I'm still learning today! That's what I want other people on the spectrum to learn: You just can't give up. You have to keep trying." The wisdom she offers through this book and its personal reflections on autism will, I'm sure, ring true for many more decades to come.

RUTH CHRIST SULLIVAN, PH.D.
May 2008

**Ruth Christ Sullivan, Ph.D.** was the first elected president of the Autism Society of America (formerly NSAC), founded in 1965 by the late Dr. Bernard Rimland. In 1979 she founded and was Executive Director of Autism Services Center (ASC), in Huntington, WV until her retirement in 2007, at age 83. ASC is a nonprofit, licensed behavioral health care agency that serves all developmental disabilities but specializes in comprehensive, autism-specific services, in community-based settings including clients' homes. ASC serves approximately 270 clients, with a staff of 350. Dr. Sullivan was one of the chief autism lobbyists for Public Law 94-142 (now known as the Individuals with Disabilities Education Act, IDEA), as well as the Developmental Disabilities Act. She was the main force behind the founding of the West Virginia Autism Training Center at Marshall University, in Huntington, WV, in 1983.

Dr. Sullivan assisted in the production of the 1988 movie, *Rain Man*, serving as a consultant on autism behavior. Dustin Hoffman, who won an Oscar for his starring role as Raymond Babbett, worked directly with Dr. Sullivan and her son, Joseph (born in 1960), who has autism, in practicing for his role. The premiere of *Rain Man* was held in Huntington with Dustin Hoffman and Barry Levinson, the producer, present. It was a benefit event for Autism Services Center.

Though Dr. Sullivan has lived in Huntington, WV for forty years, she is still close to her large, south Louisiana Cajun family in Lake Charles.

# For Readers New to Autism

A UTISM IS A DEVELOPMENTAL DISORDER, TYPICALLY DIAGNOSED during early childhood. It is neurological in nature, affecting the brain in four major areas of functioning: language/communication, social skills, sensory systems, and behavior. The causes of autism remain a mystery. Current research suggests there may be different subsets of the disorder arising from genetics, environmental insults, or a combination of both.

**Every person with autism is unique,** with a different profile of strengths and challenges. No two individuals manifest the same characteristics in the same degree of severity. It is a "spectrum" disorder, and the various individual diagnoses are collectively referred to as autism spectrum disorders (ASD). Individuals on the spectrum range from those who are nonverbal with severe challenges that can include self-injurious behaviors and mental retardation, to individuals on the higher-functioning end of the spectrum (known as Asperger's Syndrome) who are extremely intelligent, with good expressive verbal language, yet markedly impaired social skills and weak perspective-taking abilities. Proposed changes in diagnostic criteria in the DSM (Diagnostic and Statistical Manual of Mental Disorders), the diagnostic "bible" of the medical community, may eliminate Asperger's Syndrome and merge the various autism labels into one designation, "Autism Spectrum Disorders."

**The rate of autism is now 1 in every 100 births** (Centers for Disease Control, 2009) and continues to escalate at alarming rates. Every 21 minutes a child is diagnosed on the spectrum. It is four times more common in boys than girls, and is consistently prevalent around the globe, and within different racial, social, and ethnic communities. According to the Autism Society of America, the lifetime cost of caring for a single child with autism ranges from $3.5 - $5 million; the tally for all costs for all individuals approaches a staggering *$90 billion annually.*[1]

**Autism is a different way of thinking and learning.** People with autism are people first; autism is only one part of who they are. ASD is no longer viewed as strictly a behavioral disorder, but one that affects the whole person on various fronts: biomedical, cognitive, social, and sensory. With individualized and appropriate intervention, children with ASD can become more functional and learn to adapt to the world around them.

**Great strides are being made** in our understanding of autism spectrum disorders and how best to help these individuals. Children are now being diagnosed as early as 12-15 months old, and many who receive intensive early intervention are able to enter elementary school in class with their typical peers, needing minor supports and services. No matter the age of diagnosis, children and adults with ASD are constant learners and significant improvements in their functioning can be made at any age with the appropriate types and intensity of services.

(©*Autism Asperger's Digest*, 2008. Reprinted with permission)

[1] Autism Society of America website, *www.autism-society.org*

# Tony & Temple: Face to Face

T EMPLE GRANDIN'S AUTOBIOGRAPHY *EMERGENCE: LABELED AUTISTIC* and her subsequent book, *Thinking in Pictures,* together contain more information and insights into autism than I have read in any textbook. When I first heard one of her presentations, I was immediately aware of her forthright personality. The whole audience was enthralled with her knowledge.

I was delighted to be asked to interview Temple, as it provided an opportunity to seek her counsel on so many topics. She has a remarkably endearing personality and during the interview in San Francisco she entranced an audience of over 300 people. The applause at the end was loud and prolonged.

Temple is my hero. She has my vote for the person who has provided the greatest advance in our understanding of autism this century.

DR. TONY ATTWOOD
World-renowned expert on autism and Asperger's Syndrome

*Ed. Note: The following interview was taped live on December 9th, 1999 at a presentation Temple was giving in San Francisco for Future Horizons. The audience loved it! It provided many revealing, and sometimes humorous, glimpses into Temple's life. It was a rare opportunity to see Temple break into hearty laughter. Enjoy!*

**Tony:** Temple, you were diagnosed as autistic when you were fifteen years old. How did your parents present that to you and what did you feel about yourself when you got that information?

**Temple:** Well, they never really presented it properly. I sort of found out about it in a roundabout way from my aunt. You've got to remember that I'm a child of the '50s and that was a Freudian era, a totally different time. Actually, I was kind of relieved to find out there was something wrong with me. It explained why I wasn't getting along with the other kids at school and I didn't understand some of the things teenagers did—like when my roommate would swoon over the Beatles. She'd roll around on the floor squealing in front of the Ed Sullivan show. I'd think, yeah, Ringo's cute, but I wouldn't roll around on the floor with him. …

**Tony:** So, if you had the job of explaining to a fourteen- or fifteen-year-old that you have autism or Asperger's Syndrome, how would you talk about it today?

**Temple:** I think I might give them your book and my book. … Well, I'd probably just explain it in a technical manner: that it's immature development in the brain that interferes with getting along socially. I'm basically a "techie"—that's the kind of person I am. I want to fix things. With most of the things I do, I take the engineering approach; my emotions are simple. I get satisfaction out of doing good work. I get satisfaction when a parent comes to me and says "I read your book and it really helped my kid in school." I get satisfaction from what I do.

**Tony:** I seem to remember when you were very little and very autistic, there were certain autistic behaviors you really enjoyed doing. What were they?

**Temple:** One of the things I used to do was dribble sand through my hands and watch the sand, studying each little particle like a scientist looking at it under a microscope. When I did that I could tune the whole world out. You know, I think it's okay for an autistic kid to do a little bit of that, because it's calming. But if they do it all day, they're not going to develop. Lovaas' research showed that kids need forty hours a week connected to the world. I don't agree with forty hours a week of what I call "hard-core applied behavior analysis," just done at a table. But I had forty hours a week of being tuned in. I had an hour and-a-half a day of Miss Manners meals where I had to behave. Then nanny played structured children's games with me and my sister, ones that involved a lot of turn-taking. I had my speech therapy class every day ... these things were very important to my development.

Tony: A moment ago you used the word "calming." One of the problems that some persons with autism and Asperger's have is managing their temper. How do you control your temper?

Temple: When I was a little kid, if I had a temper tantrum at school, mother just said, "You're not going to watch any *Howdy Doody* show tonight." I was in a normal school—twelve kids in a class, a structured classroom. There was a lot of coordination between school and home. I knew I couldn't play mom against the teachers, or vice versa. I just knew if I had a temper tantrum there wouldn't be any TV that night. When I got into high school and kids were teasing me, I got into some rather serious fist fights. I got kicked out of the school for that—it was not good. And then when I went away to the boarding school and I got into some fist fights, they took away horseback riding privileges. Well, I wanted to ride the horses and after I had horseback-riding privileges taken away once, I stopped fighting. It was just that simple.

Tony: But can I ask you, personally, whom were you fighting, and did you win?

Temple: Well ... I usually won a lot of the fights ...

Tony: So, were you fighting the boys or the girls?

Temple: Both—the people who teased me.

Tony: So you'd actually lay out the boys?

Temple: Oh, I remember one time I punched a boy right in the cafeteria ... and then when I stopped fighting, the way I dealt with it was that I would just cry, because it's my way of preventing fighting. I also avoid situations where people are blowing up and getting angry. I just walk away from them.

**Tony:** I'd like to ask you a technical question. If you had $10 million for research and you were either going to create research in new areas, or support existing research, where would you spend that money?

**Temple:** One of the areas I would spend it on is really figuring out what causes all the sensory problems. I realize it's not the core deficit in autism, but it's something that makes it extremely difficult for persons with autism to function. Another really bad thing, especially in the high-functioning end of the spectrum, is that as the people get older, they get more and more anxious. Even if they take Prozac or something else, they're so anxious, they have a hard time functioning. I wish there was some way to control that without drugging them totally to death. Then you get into issues like, should we prevent autism? I get concerned about that because if we totally get rid of the genetics that cause autism, then we'd be getting rid of a lot of talented and gifted people, like Einstein. I think life is a continuum of normal to abnormal. After all, the really social people are not the people who make computers, who make power plants, who make big hotel buildings like this one. The social people are too busy socializing.

**Tony:** So, you wouldn't fund getting rid of Asperger's Syndrome. You don't see it as a tragedy?

**Temple:** Well, it would be nice to get rid of the causation for the severely impaired, if there was a way we could preserve some of the genetics, too. But the problem is that there are a lot of different interacting genes. If you get a little bit of the trait, it's good; you get too much of the trait, it's bad. It seems to be how genetics works. One thing I've learned from working with animals, when breeders overselect for a certain trait, you can get other bad things that come along with it. For example, with chickens, they selected for fast growth and lots of meat, but then they had problems with the skeleton not being strong enough. So they bred a strong skeleton back into the chicken. And they got a big, rude surprise they weren't expecting. They ended up with roosters that the breeding hens were attacking and slashing. When they bred the strong legs back in, it bred out the rooster's normal courtship behavior. Now, who would have predicted this strange problem? That's the way genetics works.

**Tony:** Temple, one characteristic you have is that you make people laugh. I think sometimes you may not intend it, but you have a great gift of making people laugh. What makes you laugh? What's your sense of humor?

**Temple:** Well for one thing, my humor is visually based. When I was telling you about the chickens, I was seeing pictures of them. One time I was in our department conference room at the university. They have framed pictures of all the old department heads, in heavy, thick, wooden frames. I looked at that and said, "Oh, framed geezers!" At another faculty meeting I was looking at them, and I wanted to burst out laughing, thinking about the framed geezers. That's visual humor.

**Tony:** And you have a story about pigeons?

**Temple:** Oh yeah, the pigeon stuff. Wayne and I got rolling around on the ground one night about pigeons. The Denver airport has a lot of pigeons and they don't clean up the dead pigeons in the parking lot. I got to thinking about the places I could put the dead pigeons … like a pigeon hood-ornament for all the city of Denver maintenance trucks. Then they have this place they call the pigeon drop zone. In the parking garage there's this one concrete beam where they all nest … well you don't want to park in the pigeon drop zone. Every time I walk back to the parking garage, I'm wondering what big fancy expensive $30,000 SUV just parked in the pigeon drop zone.

**Tony:** So, that explains why sometimes you may burst into laughter and other people have no idea what's going on. …

**Temple:** That's right; it's because I'm looking at a picture in my mind of something that's funny … I can just see that pigeon hood-ornament on a bright yellow Denver city truck—it's just very funny.

**Tony:** About your family: your mother was a very important part of your life. What sort of a person is she? What did she do personally that helped you?

**Temple:** She kept me out of an institution, first of all. You've got to remember this was fifty years ago; all of the professionals recommended that I be put into an institution. Mother took me to a really good neurologist and the neurologist recommended the speech therapy nursery school. That was just a piece of luck. The nursery school was run by two teachers out of their house. They had six kids and they weren't all autistic. They were just good teachers who knew how to work with kids. They hired the nanny, when I was three, and the nanny had had experience working with autistic kids. I have a feeling the nanny might have been Asperger's herself, because she had an old car seat out of a jeep that she had in her room—it was her favorite chair.

**Tony:** How else did your mother help you as a person herself?

**Temple:** Well, she worked with me a lot. She encouraged my interest in art; she did some drawing things with me. She had worked as a journalist, putting together a TV show on mentally disabled persons and then another TV program on emotionally disturbed children. Of course, back then, fifty years ago, different children were all labeled as emotionally disturbed. As a journalist, she had gone out and visited different schools. So when I got into trouble in ninth grade for throwing a book at a girl—I got kicked out of the school and we had to find another school—she found a boarding school that was one of the schools she had visited as a journalist. If she hadn't done that for me, I don't know what would have happened. Once I got into the boarding school, that's when I found people like my science teacher and my

Aunt Ann, out on the ranch, who were other important mentors. But there were a lot of people along the way who helped me.

Tony: What about your father? Describe your father and grandfather.

Temple: My grandfather on my mother's side invented the automatic pilot for airplanes. He was very shy and quiet; he wasn't very social. On my father's side of the family we have temper problems. My father didn't think I would amount to very much. He wasn't very social either.

Tony: How do you relax? What do you do to calm down at the end of the day?

Temple: Before I took medication I used to watch *Star Trek*—I was very much a Trekkie. One of the things I liked, especially about the old classic *Star Trek*, was that it always had good moral principles. I'm very concerned today about all the violent stuff. It isn't so much how many guns are going off in the movies, it's that the hero doesn't have good values. When I was a little kid, Superman and the Lone Ranger never did anything that was wrong. Today, we have heroes that do things like throw the woman into the water or the woman ends up getting shot; the hero is supposed to be protecting the woman, not letting her get shot. You don't have clear-cut values. And this worries me, because my morals are determined by logic. What would my logic and morals have become if I hadn't been watching those programs, with clear-cut moral principles?

Tony: As we turn to the next millennium, in another 100 years time, how do you think our understanding of autism will change?

Temple: Oh, I don't know … we'll probably have total genetic engineering and they'll have a Windows 3000 "Make a Person" program. They'll know how to read DNA code by then. We don't know how to do that right now. Scientists can manipulate DNA—take it out and put it in—but they cannot read the four-base source code. One hundred years from now they'll be able to do that. And, I don't think there will be autism, at least not the severe forms of it, because we'll be able to totally manipulate the DNA by then.

**Tony:** There are a number of persons we've learned about now with autism or Asperger's Syndrome who have written their autobiographies. Who are your heroes in the autism/Asperger's field who have the condition themselves?

**Temple:** I really look to the people who have made a success of themselves. There's a lady named Sara Miller; she programs industrial computers for factory automation. There's a lady here tonight, very beautifully dressed, who has her own jewelry business, and she told me she has Asperger's. Somebody like that is my hero … somebody who's making a success of himself or herself, who is getting out there and doing things.

**Tony:** How about famous people historically, who would you think had autism or Asperger's Syndrome?

**Temple:** I think Einstein had a lot of autistic traits. He didn't talk until age three—I have a whole chapter about Einstein in my last book. I think Thomas Jefferson had some Asperger's traits. Bill Gates has tremendous memory. I remember reading in an article that he memorized the whole Torah as a child. It's a continuum—there's just no black and white dividing line between a computer techie and say, an Asperger's person. They just all blend right together. So if we get rid of the genetics that cause autism, there might be a horrible price to pay. Years ago, a scientist in Massachusetts said if you got rid of all the genes that caused disorders, you'd have only dried up bureaucrats left!

*To conclude, Tony opened up the interview to questions from the audience. Here's one of the best.*

**Audience member:** How did you realize you had control over your life?

**Temple:** I was not a good student in high school; I did a lot of fooling around. Being a visual thinker, I had to use door symbolism—an actual physical door that I would practice walking through—to symbolize that I was going on to the next step in my life. When you think visually, and you don't have very much stuff on the [mental] hard drive from previous experiences, you've got to have something to use as a visual map. My science teacher got me motivated with different science projects and I realized if I wanted to go to college and become a scientist, I'd have to study. Well, one day I made myself walk through this one door and I said, "Okay, I'm going to try to study during French class." But there was a point where I realized that I had to do some things about my own behavior. And I had experienced some times that were not all that easy, like when my boss got all over me for being a total slob. There were mentors who forced me—and it wasn't always pleasant—but they forced me to realize that I had to change my behavior. People on the spectrum just can't be sitting around complaining about things. They have to actively try to change things. Good mentors can help you do that.

A clinical psychologist from Brisbane, Australia, Dr. Tony Attwood has over thirty years of experience with individuals with autism, Asperger's Syndrome, and Pervasive Developmental Disorder (PDD). He has worked with several thousand individuals, from infants to octogenarians, from profoundly disabled persons to university professors. His books and videos on Asperger's Syndrome and high-functioning autism are recognized as the best offerings in the field. Over 300,000 copies of his book *Asperger's Syndrome: A Guide for Parents and Professionals,* have been sold, and it has been translated into twenty languages.

# Introduction

THIS BOOK IS A COMPILATION OF ARTICLES I HAVE WRITTEN FOR THE *Autism Asperger's Digest* magazine from 2000 to the present. The articles have been grouped into different categories, addressing subjects from early educational interventions, to sensory sensitivity problems, to brain research and careers. At the beginning of each section I have added a new, updated introduction, which includes additional thoughts on the subject matter.

The articles combine both my personal experiences with autism and practical information that parents, teachers, and individuals on the autism spectrum can put to immediate use. The autism spectrum is very broad, ranging from individuals who remain nonverbal to a mild Asperger's individual who is a brilliant scientist or computer engineer. This book contains information that can be applied across the entire autism spectrum.

# CHAPTER ONE

# Diagnosis and Early Intervention

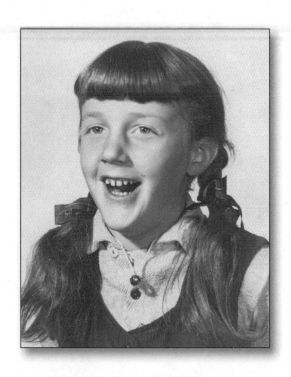

The best thing a parent of a
newly diagnosed child can
do is to watch their child,
without preconceived
notions and judgments,
and learn how the child functions,
acts, and reacts to his or her world.

B OTH RESEARCH AND PRACTICAL EXPERIENCE SHOW THAT AN INTEN-sive early education program, in which a young child receives a minimum of twenty hours a week of instruction from a skilled teacher, greatly improves prognosis. The brain of the young child is still growing and evolving. At this age, the neural pathways are highly malleable, and intensive instruction can reprogram "faulty wiring" that prevents the child from learning. Plus, behaviors in a young child have not yet become ingrained. It will take less practice to change an inappropriate behavior at age two to three than it will to change that same behavior at age seven to eight. By then, the child has had many years of doing things his way, and change comes about more slowly.

ABA (Applied Behavioral Analysis) programs using discrete trial training have the best scientific documentation backing up their use, but other programs are also effective. The autism spectrum is vast and diversified. Children have different ways of thinking and processing information, and it is important that an intervention method be aligned with the child's learning profile and personality. Detailed descriptions of different types of early intervention programs can be found in a book I recommend: *Early Intervention & Autism: Real-life Questions, Real-life Answers* by Dr. James Ball (2008, Future Horizons, Inc.). While this book is written for parents of newly diagnosed children, more than three-quarters of the information on interventions, effective teaching strategies, program planning, and behavior management is valuable for parents of children of all ages.

## My Early Intervention Program

I had a wonderful, effective early education program that started at age two and a half. By then, I had all the classic symptoms of autism: no speech, no eye contact, tantrums, and constant repetitive behavior. In

1949, the doctors knew nothing about autism, but my mother would not accept that nothing could be done to help me. She was determined, and knew that letting me continue to exist as I was, would be the worst thing she could do. On her own, she found good teachers to work with me—professionals who back then were just as good as the autism specialists today. A talented speech therapist worked with me for three hours a week doing ABA-type training (breaking skills down into small components, teaching each component separately, using repetitive drills that gave me lots of practice) and she carefully enunciated hard consonant sounds so I could hear them. At the speech therapy school, I also attended a highly structured nursery school class with five or six other children who were not autistic. Several of the children had Down Syndrome. These classes lasted about eight hours a week. My nanny was another critical part of my early therapy. She spent twenty hours a week keeping me engaged, for instance, playing repeated turn-taking games with my sister and me. She was instrumental in introducing early social skills lessons, even though at that time they weren't referred to as such in a formal manner. Within the realm of play, she kept me engaged and set up activities so that most involved turn-taking and lessons about being with others. In the winter, we went outdoors to play in the snow. She brought one sled, and my sister and I had to take turns sledding down the hill. In the summer, we took turns on the swing. We also were taught to sit at the table and have good table manners. Teaching and learning opportunities were woven into everyday life. When I turned five, we played lots of board games such as Parcheesi and Chinese checkers. My interest in art and making things was actively encouraged and I did many art projects. For most of the day I was forced to keep my brain tuned into the world. However, my mother realized that my behaviors served a purpose and that changing those behaviors didn't happen overnight, but gradually. I was given one hour after lunch where I could revert back to autistic behaviors without consequence. During this hour I had to stay in my room, and I sometimes spent the entire time spinning a decorative brass plate that covered a bolt that held my bed frame together. I would spin it at different speeds and was fascinated at how different speeds affected the number of times the brass plate spun.

The best thing a parent of a newly diagnosed child can do is to watch their child, without preconceived notions and judgments, and learn how the child functions, acts, and reacts to his or her world. That information will be invaluable in finding an intervention method that will be a good match to the child's learning style and needs. The worst thing parents can do with a child between the ages of 2-5 is *nothing*. It doesn't matter if the child is formally diagnosed with autism, PDD-NOS or has been labeled something less defined, like global developmental delay. It doesn't matter if the child is not yet diagnosed, but something is obviously "wrong"—speech is severely delayed, the child's behaviors are odd and repetitive, the child doesn't engage with people or his environment. The child must not be allowed to sit around stimming all day or conversely, tuning out from the world around him. Parents, hear this: **Doing nothing is the worst thing you can do**. If you have a three-year-old with no speech who is showing signs of autistic behavior, you need to start working with your child NOW. If signs are appearing in a child younger than three, even better. Do not wait six more months or a year, even if your pediatrician is suggesting you take the "wait and see" approach, or is plying you with advice such as "Boys develop later than girls," or "Not all children start to speak at the same time." My advice to act now is doubly emphasized if your child's language started developing on time and his language and/or behavior is *regressing*.

Parents can find themselves on long waiting lists for both diagnosis and early intervention services. In some cases, the child will age out of the state's early intervention system (birth to three) before his name gets to the top of the list! There is much parents can do to begin working with the child before formal professional intervention begins. Play turn-taking games and encourage eye contact. Grandmothers who have lots of experience with children can be very effective. *Engagement* with the child at this point in time is just as effective as is instruction. While you may not be (yet) knowledgeable about various autism intervention models, you *are* smart enough and motivated enough to engage your child for 20 plus hours a week. **Don't wait; act now.**

ADDITIONAL READING

Ball, J. 2008. *Early intervention & autism: Real-life questions, real-life answers.* Arlington, TX: Future Horizons, Inc.

Grandin, T. 1996. *Emergence: Labeled autistic.* New York: Warner Books.

Koegel, L., and C. Lazebnik. 2004. *Overcoming autism: Finding strategies and hope that can transform a child's life.* New York: Penguin Group.

# Do Not Get
# Hung Up on Labels

D IAGNOSES FOR DISEASES SUCH AS TUBERCULOSIS OR CANCER ARE precise. Lab tests can tell you the exact types of disease you have. Unfortunately, a diagnosis for autism, Asperger's Syndrome or PDD-NOS (pervasive developmental disorder, not otherwise speci-fied) lacks the precision of medical tests for cancer. There are no lab tests or brain scans that can be used to definitively diagnose autism spectrum disorders. In the future, precise tests may become available but none exist today.

A diagnosis of a developmental disorder is based on a *behavioral* profile described in the "doctor's manual" most physicians use: the DSM-IV (Diagnostic Manual of Mental Disorders, 4th edition), pub-lished by the American Psychiatric Association[1]. In making a diagnosis, doctors consult the manual to see what diagnosis best fits the behav-ioral profile of the child. Diagnosis of developmental disorders is a subjective process, and the DSM-IV is just one tool, among many, that a doctor should rely upon. Many conditions have overlapping symp-toms, and the experience of the physician can have a huge impact on the accuracy of the diagnosis. For instance, a doctor who specializes in autism spectrum disorders, one who sees a vast range of individuals of different ages and at different stages of development, would be far more

[1]This chapter will cover both the existing DSM IV guidelines and the proposed
    DSM V revisions that will take effect in 2013.

qualified to diagnose a child on the spectrum than a general pediatrician in a rural area whose familiarity with ASD extends to less than a handful of individuals. There is often disagreement between psychologists and medical doctors on diagnosis, and some clinicians deviate from the guidelines in the DSM-IV based on their experiences. Some doctors even refrain from making an autism diagnosis because of the emotional impact they fear it will have on the parents.

For a child to be correctly diagnosed with *autism* the child must have delayed or no speech coupled with other impairments in the areas of behavior, social skills, and play skills. Among the behaviors that indicate autism are lack of eye contact, repetitive behaviors such as hand-flapping or rocking, and avoidance of or little interest in social interaction. These symptoms must occur before age three and be obvious enough that the child's functioning is markedly different than his typical peers'. Children who fit the diagnostic criteria for *PDD-NOS* have the same early onset of symptoms, but they often display fewer autistic behaviors or display them in milder forms. *Asperger's Syndrome* is a milder variant on the autism continuum, with the one main difference being that these children have no obvious speech delay. These individuals, too, exist on a spectrum of abilities, and can be easily overlooked because of their language skills and, often, advanced intelligence, especially in one area. However, their sensory problems and pervasive social impairments are usually obvious, to the trained eye. They are often loners, with few friends, the geeks, the nerds, the socially odd individuals who never seem to fit in. While the average age of diagnosis of autism or PDD-NOS is between three and four years old, children are often not diagnosed with Asperger's until they are eight or nine. Many are misdiagnosed with conditions that share many of the same characteristics, such as ADHD, learning disabilities, or dyslexia. I also want to emphasize that as therapy helps a child improve, a diagnosis is sometimes changed, and in some cases, children can make such progress that they lose their label. However, autism or Asperger's Syndrome is a lifelong condition arising from biomedical, brain-based origins; it never goes away.

---------------------------------------------------------------

There is much controversy about the alarming increase in autism spectrum disorders over the last 10-15 years. Some of this increase is undoubtedly due to broadening the spectrum of autism diagnoses. The addition of Asperger's Syndrome as an "official" diagnosis for education services appeared just in 1994, and since then our awareness of the disorder in both children and adults has skyrocketed as we learn more about this population of individuals. Pediatricians are more aware of autism spectrum disorders now, as are parents, who are more vocal in expressing their concerns with their doctors when something is just not "right" with their child. Despite increased awareness and a broader spectrum of conditions to be diagnosed, I still think there has been a true increase in what is called *regressive autism.* In classic autism, the warning signs are present from birth. With regressive autism, however, a child is meeting most typical developmental milestones in speech, motor skills and social development, and then loses functioning somewhere at age 18-24 months. Geraldine Dawson, at the University of Washington, has documented the existence of this regressive form of autism by analyzing videos of children's birthday parties. Other autism-savvy researchers who specialize in the early warning signs of ASD, such as Dr. Rebecca Landa of the Kennedy Krieger Institute at Johns Hopkins University in Baltimore, MD, are noticing the same regression. Why this is happening has yet to be determined. Our best guess to date is that these children are born with compromised immune systems then subjected to an environmental insult or combination of insults that opens the door for the autism expression.

The autism spectrum is very broad, ranging from an individual who remains completely nonverbal into adulthood to a brilliant scientist with Asperger's Syndrome who continues to struggle with understanding the social nuances of the world. However the child comes to the diagnosis of autism or PDD-NOS or Asperger's Syndrome, I want to warn parents and teachers: **Do not get hung up on labels.** Labels are useful for obtaining services, to grant a child eligibility into programs or for financial aid services. But the label should never define the child, nor dictate what program should be used with a child. Autism spectrum disorders are varied and no two individuals will manifest the same set of characteristics at the same level of intensity. Always look at the child—not the label—and base treatment decisions on the child's individual profile of strengths and weaknesses, learning style, personality, etc. It would be easier for parents and educators if, as with cancer or diabetes, we could equate the label with a proven form of treatment. Diagnosed with autism? Use treatment programs X, Y, or Z. Diagnosed with Asperger's? Instead use program C, D, or E. That is not the case; it may never be the case. Far too often we adults make gross assumptions about the capabilities of people with ASD based on their label, especially with children who are nonverbal or have limited verbal abilities. **NEVER** let a label lower your reasonable expectations of a child and that child's capacity for learning. By doing so, you rob the child of the very experiences and opportunities that can allow learning to grow and develop. You rob the child of his potential, and his future. All because of a label?

The boundaries that separate the developmental disorders are fuzzy and imprecise. There are no black and white dividing lines between autism, PDD-NOS, and Asperger's Syndrome. It is a very broad spectrum and the more we learn about these individuals, the greater appreciation we have for the myriad strengths and challenges they display. Let us not limit the lives of these children and adults by our own preconceived notions based on the label attached to them. See the person, not the label.

## Diagnosis Update 2010

The American Psychiatric Association, author of the DSM, is proposing a major revision of the DSM-IV manual, to take effect in 2013. Within the category Pervasive Developmental Disorders, the current umbrella under which the various forms of autism are included, they propose elimination of both the Asperger and PDD-NOS labels and merging them into a single diagnostic category called "Autistic Spectrum

Disorder." To be labeled with Autistic Spectrum Disorder in the proposed DSM-V, symptoms must be present in early childhood; however, the age of onset is no longer defined. There are no specific criteria for the presence of speech delay. The proposed guideline whittles symptoms down to major areas: social and behavioral. It emphasizes the social abnormalities inherent in the disorder. And, the child must have two out of three abnormal behaviors, such as stereotyped (repetitive) motor or verbal behaviors, rigid routines or ritualized patterns of behavior, or restricted, fixed interests. On the positive side, the proposed guidelines acknowledge the widespread sensory sensitivities of individuals on the autism spectrum, something that, up until now, was not included in the diagnosis. "Unusual sensory behaviors" is proposed for inclusion as a behavioral manifestation.

Compared to the present DSM criteria, the new guidelines are very vague. Unfortunately, this may open the door to practitioners using the guidelines to their advantage, rather than to the advantage of the child needing help. I have observed that some school systems may already be using these proposed revisions to avoid the autism label, and label children who manifest these symptoms as either Emotional Disorder (ED), Oppositional Defiant Disorder (ODD), or Temper Dysregulation Disorder (TDD). According to the proposed guidelines, children can be labeled with TDD when they are six years of age or older. Its main symptom is frequent temper outbursts. The ODD label can be used in children of all ages. Its main symptoms are active defiance, vindictiveness, and sustained anger. These are all overlapping symptoms with ASD, however, the needs of children with ASD extend into areas not addressed by these other labels.

My concern is that children who need autism services will get shunted off into other labels so that less money will be required for services. School systems on shrinking budgets may be more and more likely to do this. In the end, it is these children who suffer. However, the long-term, and frightening, consequence will be the millions, if not billions, of dollars in tax-payer revenue needed to support these children when they become adults. Appropriate services for these children while they are young is a cost-effective measure for everyone in the long run.

## REFERENCE

American Psychiatric Association. 1994. *Diagnostic and statistical manual IV*, Washington, D.C.

American Psychiatric Association. 2010. *Proposed revision for the DSM V.* www.dsm5.org accessed December 22, 2010.

# Economical Quality
# Programs for Young
# Children with ASD

I WAS LUCKY TO GET STATE-OF-THE-ART EARLY INTERVENTION (EI) AND education while growing up in the early 1950s. Despite the lack of knowledge about autism and how to treat it (aside from institutionalization, which was the norm at that time), my mother had me in an excellent speech therapy nursery school by age three and I had a nanny who spent hours and hours per week playing turn-taking games and structured, enjoyable activities with me. In addition, our household's behavior rules were well-defined and social manners and social expectations were strictly enforced. Fortunately, my parents had enough money to pay for the programs that contributed to my development and laid the foundations for successful functioning as I grew up and ventured out on my own. Adjusting the fees for inflation, the cost of my program would probably be in the mid-range, compared to early intervention programs being used today. Many programs now available are much more expensive.

Can parents on a limited budget put together a good program for their young autistic child? The answer is yes, with a little thought and planning. I have talked to parents who have put together their own successful EI program after reading a few books and enlisting the help of volunteers. Self-motivation and an unfailing desire to help their child are needed as much as is education about autism. The absolute worst thing a parent can do is to let their child sit and watch TV all day or zone out unaware of his or her surroundings. This is precious time wasted, never to be regained.

Both research and practical experience has indicated that twenty or more hours of intense one-to-one interaction with an effective teacher and/or adult can kick-start speech and improve language and other behaviors in children with ASD. In many parts of the country a public school will provide only one or two hours a week of therapy with a speech therapist, an occupational therapist (OT), or a behavioral specialist. This is not enough to be really effective, but it does present an opportunity for training of the individuals who work with the child outside of the school day. This is especially true for parents, who need to take the lead and provide supplemental instruction themselves.

I recommend that parents in those situations approach the school therapists as "coaches" who can educate them about their child's autism and teach them how to do more intensive therapy at home. It also helps if family members or volunteers who are working with the child (for instance, a grandmother who has volunteered to work with a four year old) visit the school every week and watch the professional therapist work with the child. The professionals can give volunteers therapy assignments to work on with the child during the week. Invaluable information can be gleaned by watching sessions "in action" that no amount of reading will ever convey. Conversely, it might also be helpful from time to time to pay the therapist to spend an hour or two observing how the in-home program is unfolding. Sometimes a small change to a program can make a world of difference and it often takes a trained eye to spot situations like this. The weekly get-togethers are also a perfect time to discuss the child's progress and review goals and objectives for the coming week so everyone can keep track of progress and program changes.

Church and civic groups are a great place to find people who might be willing to work with a child. Other sources of help include students from the local high school or college students. When looking for volunteers to help teach the child, try to be specific about the types of things they will be doing. For instance, grandmothers might feel comfortable volunteering to "play" with a child, or help provide "simple structured, repetitive drills"—those are familiar skills most people possess. Yet the same grandmother might feel ill-equipped if you ask them to "help out with the therapeutic behavior program designed for a child with autism." Most people don't know what that type of program entails, and they may think that only someone with a college degree would have relevant skills. Be sure to mention that you (or someone else) will be providing them with basic education and training on autism to further reinforce their ability to handle what comes up. Many people are genuinely interested in helping others, provided they get some training on how to do it.

I have observed that some teachers and therapists have a knack for working with children with ASD and others do not. Passive approaches do not work. Parents need to find the people, both professionals and non-professionals, who know how to be gently insistent, who keep the child motivated to learn, are child-centered in their approach, and are dedicated to teaching children with autism in a way they can learn, instead of insisting the child learn in the way they teach. Doing so naturally engages the child, which is the foundation of any effective program for children with autism, no matter what the cost.

Strategies that build on
the child's area of strength
and appeal to their thinking
patterns will be most effective.

# Different Types of
# Thinking in Autism

RECENT STUDIES ON THE BRAIN, AND ESPECIALLY ON THE BRAINS OF people diagnosed with autism spectrum disorders, are shedding light on the physiological underpinnings of our thoughts and emotions. We are gaining a better understanding of how neural pathways are formed and the extent to which biology influences behavior.

When I was much younger, I assumed that everybody perceived the world the same way I did, that is, that everybody thought in pictures. Early in my professional career I got into a heated verbal argument with an engineer at a meat-packing plant when I told him he was stupid. He had designed a piece of equipment that had flaws that were obvious to me. My visual thinking gives me the ability to do a "test-run" in my head on a piece of equipment I've designed, just like a virtual reality computer system. Mistakes can be found prior to construction when I do this. Now I realize his problem was not stupidity; it was a lack of visual thinking. It took me years to learn that the majority of people cannot do this, and that visualization skills in some people are almost nonexistent.

All minds on the autism/Asperger's spectrum are detail-oriented, but how they specialize varies. By questioning many people, both on and off the spectrum, I have learned that there are three different types of specialized thinking with crossover among these specialized thinking patterns. Determining thinking types in three-year-old children is often not possible. Dominant thinking styles usually become more obvious when a child is seven to nine.

- Visual thinking/thinking in photo realistic pictures, like mine
- Music and Math thinking in patterns
- Verbal thinking (not a visual thinker)

Since autism is so variable, there may be mixtures of the different types. For instance, a child may have strong music/math patterned thinking, but also have good visual thinking abilities. Or a verbal thinker may also have good math or foreign-language skills. The importance of understanding these three ways of thinking comes into play when trying to teach children with ASD. Strategies that build on the child's area of strength and appeal to their thinking patterns will be most effective. This is most likely to become evident between the ages of five and eight. It is often difficult to identify the strengths of children younger than five, unless savant skills are unfolding.

## Visual Thinkers

These children often love art and building blocks, such as Legos, and they will often produce beautiful drawings. They get easily immersed in projects that have a tangible, hands-on opportunity for learning. Math concepts such as adding and subtracting need to be taught starting with concrete objects the child can touch. Drawing and other art skills should be encouraged. If a child only draws one thing, such as airplanes, encourage him to draw other related objects, such as the airport runways, or the hangars, or cars going to the airport. Broadening a child's emerging skills helps him be more flexible in his thinking patterns. Keep in mind that because the child's "native language" is pictures, verbal responses can take longer to form, as each request has to be translated from words to pictures before it can be processed, and then the response needs to be translated from pictures into words before it is spoken. Visual thinkers often have difficulty doing algebra because of its abstract nature, but some can do geometry and trigonometry quite easily. Visual thinkers often find success in careers as artists, graphic designers, photographers, or industrial engineers.

## Music and Math Thinkers

Patterns instead of pictures dominate the thinking processes of these children. Both music and math are a world of patterns, and children who think this way can have strong associative abilities. They like finding relationships between numbers or musical notes; some children may have savant-type calculation skills or be able to play a piece of music after hearing it just once. Musical talent often emerges without formal instruction. Many of these children can teach themselves if keyboards and other instruments are available. When they grow up, pattern thinkers are often very good at computer programming, engineering, or music. Some of these children should be advanced several grades ahead in math, depending on their abilities, but they may need special education in reading, which may lag behind.

## Verbal Thinkers

These children love lists and numbers. Often they will memorize bus timetables and events in history. Interest areas often include history, geography, weather, and sports statistics. They are not visual thinkers. Parents and teachers can use these interests and talents as motivation for learning less-interesting parts of academics. Some verbal thinkers are whizzes at learning many different foreign languages. I know individuals with verbal thinking skills who have been successfully employed in sales, stage acting, accounting, factual/technical writing, and pharmacology.

The thinking patterns of individuals with ASD are markedly different from the way "normal" people think. Because of this, too much emphasis is placed on what they "can't do" and opportunities to capitalize on their different, but often creative and novel, ways of thinking fall by the wayside. While impairments and challenges do exist, greater progress can be made teaching these individuals when parents and teachers work on building the child's strengths and teach in a manner aligned with their basic pattern of thinking.

## ADDITIONAL READING

Chiang, H. M. and Y. H. Lin. 2007. Mathematical ability of students with Asperger syndrome and high-functioning autism. *Autism* 11: 547-556.

Grandin, T. 2009. How does visual thinking work in the mind of a person with autism? A personal account. Philosophical Transactions of the Royal Society, London, UK 364:1437-1442.

Hegarty, M. and M. Kozhevnikov. 1999. Types of visual-spatial representations and mathematical problem solving. *Journal of Educational Psychology* 91: 684-689.

Jones, C. R. G. et al. 2009. Reading and arithmetic in adolescents with autism spectrum disorders: Peaks and dips in attainment. *Neuropsychology* 23: 718-728.

Mazard, A. et al. 2004. A PET meta-analysis of object and spatial mental imagery. *European Journal of Cognitive Psychology* 16: 673-695.

# Higher Expectations Yield Results

YOUNG CHILDREN WITH AUTISM SPECTRUM DISORDERS DO NOT learn by listening to and watching others, as do typical children. They need to be specifically taught things that others seem to learn by osmosis. A good teacher is gently insistent with a young autistic child in order to get progress. The teacher has to be careful not to cause sensory overload, but at the same time has to be somewhat intrusive into the child's world of stimming or silent withdrawal in order for the child to engage in learning.

When children get a little older, they need to be exposed to many different things to stimulate their continued learning in different areas of life. There also need to be expectations for proper social behavior. When I look back at my life, my mother made me do a number of things I did not like, but these activities were really beneficial. They gave me opportunities to practice social skills, converse with less-familiar people, develop self-esteem and learn to negotiate unanticipated changes. None of these activities caused major problems with sensory oversensitivity. While Mother may have pushed me to do things, she understood well that a child should never be forced into a situation that includes painful sensory stimulation.

By age five, I was required to dress up and behave in church and sit through formal dinners both at home and at Granny's. When I didn't, there was a consequence, and I lost a privilege that meant something to me. Fortunately, our church had a beautiful old-fashioned organ I liked. Most of the service was boring to me, but that organ made it somewhat tolerable to sit through. A modern church with loud, amplified music probably would be sensory overload to someone like me.

When I was reluctant to learn to ride a bike, I was urged to learn. Mother was always testing the limits on how far she could push me. I became motivated to learn after I missed a bike trip to the Coca-Cola plant.

When I was a teenager, the opportunity arose for me to visit my aunt's ranch in Arizona. At the time, I was having non-stop panic attacks and was afraid to go. Mother made me go anyway, telling me I could come home in two weeks. When I got there, I loved it and stayed all summer. Aunt Ann became one of my important mentors. My career in livestock equipment design would have never started if I had been allowed to stay home.

I often needed a certain amount of pushing to do new things by myself. I was good at building things, but afraid to go to the lumber yard and buy the wood by myself. Mother made me do it. She never let my autism be an excuse for not trying something she knew would be beneficial for me to learn. I came back crying from that outing, but I had the wood with me. Further trips to the lumber yard were easy. At one of my early jobs my boss made me "cold call" cattle magazines to get articles published. After I got over the initial fear, I found I was good at getting articles into national cattle publications. In all of the above cases, either my mother or a boss had to push me to do things even though I was afraid. Yet the things I learned—especially about myself—were priceless.

After I started my freelance design business, I almost gave it up because an early client was not 100% satisfied. My black-and-white thinking led me to believe that clients would always be 100% satisfied. Fortunately, my good friend Jim Uhl, the contractor who built my systems, would not let me quit. He actively kept pushing and talking to me and asking for the next drawing. When I produced a new drawing, he praised it. Now I know that 100% client satisfaction is impossible.

My life and career could have been derailed and wrecked if my mother and business associates had not *pushed* me to do things. Mother did not let me lie around the house, and never viewed my autism as rendering me incapable. Business associates stayed after me and made me do things. These adult mentors are a grown-up version of a good special education teacher who is gently insistent with a three-year-old child with autism. What it demonstrates overall is that people with ASD can learn and succeed when others around them believe in their abilities and hold high expectations of them.

CHAPTER TWO

# Teaching and
# Education

Good teachers understand
that for a child to learn,
the teaching style
must match the student's
learning style.

E VERY CHILD WITH ASD HAS HIS OR HER OWN PERSONALITY AND profile of strengths and weaknesses; this is no different than with typical children. They can be introverts or extroverts, have a sunny disposition or be cranky, love music or math. Parents and educators can easily forget this, and attribute every action or reaction of the child to autism or Asperger's, and therefore in need of dissection and "fixing." The way I see it, the goal in teaching children with autism is not to turn them into clones of their typical peers (i.e., "normal"). When you think about it, not all characteristics exhibited by typical people are worthy of being modeled. A much more meaningful perspective is to teach this population the academic and interpersonal skills they need to be *functional* in the world and use their talents to the best of their ability. Autism is not a death sentence for a child or the family. It brings with it great challenges, but it can also bring to the child the seeds of great talents and unique abilities. It is the responsibility of parents and educators to find those seeds, nurture them, and make sure they grow. That should be the goal of teaching and education for children with ASD too, not just for typical children.

The different thinking patterns of individuals with ASD require parents and educators to teach from a new frame of reference, one aligned with their autism way of thinking. Expecting children with ASD to learn via the conventional curriculum and teaching methods that "have always worked" for typical children is to set everyone up for failure right from the start. It would be like placing a young child on a grown up's chair and expecting his feet to reach the floor. That's just silly, isn't it? Yet, surprisingly, that is still how many schools and educators approach students with ASD. Good teachers understand that for a child to learn, the teaching style must match the student's learning style. With autism and especially with Asperger's students, it is not enough to match the teaching style to the child's learning style. Educators must take this idea one step further, and be continuously mindful that students with ASD come to school without a developed social thinking framework. This is the aspect of ASD that can be difficult for adults to understand, envision, and work around. Our public education system is built upon the premise that children enter school with basic social functioning skills in place. Kids with autism—with their characteristic social thinking challenges—enter school already lagging far behind their classmates. Teachers who don't recognize this, and make accommodations to teach social thinking and social skills alongside traditional academics, just further limit the opportunities children with ASD have to learn and grow.

## To Mainstream or Not to Mainstream?

At age five I started attending a small school with typical children. In today's language, that would be called mainstreaming. It is important to note that this worked for me because the structure and composition of the class was well matched to my needs. The school had highly structured old-fashioned classes with only twelve students. Children were expected to behave and there were strict rules, enforced consistently, and with consequences applied for infractions. The environment was relatively quiet and controlled, without a high degree of sensory stimulation. In this environment I did not need an aide. Contrast that classroom with today's learning environment. In a class of thirty students, with a single teacher, in a less structured classroom within a larger school, I would never have survived without the direct assistance of a one-on-one aide.

Whether or not to mainstream an elementary school child on the autism spectrum is a decision that should take many factors into consideration. After countless discussions with parents and teachers, I have come to the conclusion that much depends on the particular school and the particular teachers in that school. The idea of mainstreaming is a worthy goal, and in an ideal situation—where all the variables are working in favor of the child with ASD—it can be a highly positive experience. But the reality of the situation is often the opposite: lack of teacher training, large classes, limited opportunities for individual modifications, and lack of funding to support one-on-one paraprofessionals can render this environment disastrous for the spectrum child. For elementary school children on the higher functioning end of the autism spectrum, I usually favor mainstreaming because it is essential for them to learn social skills from typically developing children. If a child is homeschooled or goes to a special school, it is imperative that the child has regular engagement with typical peers. For nonverbal children, mainstreaming works well in some situations— again, much depends on the school, its expertise in autism, and its program. A special school may be a better choice for the nonverbal or cognitively impaired child with autism, especially in cases where severe, disruptive behavior problems exist and need to be addressed.

Parents frequently ask me whether or not they should change the school or program their child is in. My response is to ask this question: "Is your child making progress and improving where he is now?" If they say he is, I usually recommend staying in the school or the program and then discuss whether some additional services or program modifications may be needed. For instance, the child may do even better with more attention to physical exercise, or addressing his sensory problems, or adding a few more hours of individualized ABA (Applied Behavior Analysis) therapy or social skills training. However, if the child is making little or no progress, and the school's attitude is not supportive or accommodating of the different needs and learning styles of children with ASD so the parent is constantly battling for even the most basic services, it may be best to find a different school or program. This will, of course, require time and effort on the part of the parent, but it is important for parents to keep the end goal in sight—giving the child as much opportunity to learn and acquire needed skills in as supportive an environment as possible. It does no one good, and least of all the child, for a parent to repeatedly fight a school system, either within IEP meetings or through due process, to win their case within an environment of individuals who are not interested in truly helping the child. Sadly, this scenario plays out in schools and districts across the country. Valuable time that could be spent in meaningful instruction that helps the child is wasted while the school and parent butt heads for not just months, but in many cases, *years*. The child—and the child's needs—should always remain the focus. If the school is not child-focused, then parents should find one that is.

I reiterate a point made earlier: so much depends on the *particular people* working with the child. In one case, a third grader in a good school with an excellent reputation had several teachers who simply did not like him, nor did they attempt to understand his learning style and modify instruction to meet that style. The child hated going to school. I suggested the parents try to find a different school. They did, and the child is now doing great in his new school. In my conversations with parents and teachers, I have also observed that it doesn't matter whether the elementary school is public or private; this is seldom the issue. More depends on local conditions: the school's perception of children with disabilities and philosophy towards their education, the extent to which staff have been trained/receive ongoing training on autism spectrum disorders and how best to work with this population, and the support provided by administration to staff in educating these students. Decisions must be made on a case-by-case basis.

## The Parent Guilt Trip

It is unfortunate, but a reality of today's society, that some individuals and companies who run special schools, sell therapy services, or market products to the autism community often try to put parents on a guilt trip. All parents want what's best for their child, and parents of newly diagnosed children can be especially vulnerable. These vendors prey upon parents' emotions in advertising and personal encounters, suggesting that parents are not good parents if they don't try their program or product, or that by not using whatever it is they offer, the parent isn't doing "everything possible" to help their child. Some go as far as to tell parents that their child is doomed unless they use their program or product. One parent called me about a situation just like this. The family was ready to sell their house to have the funds needed to send their four-year-old child with autism to a special school in another state. I asked him if the child was learning and making progress at the local public school. The dad told me he was. Yet, the special school was making great claims about the progress their child would make with them. I talked with the dad about the negative impact disrupting the child's life like this might have, taking him away from his family and familiar surroundings, and sending him to a school in another state. The very real possibility existed that the child could get worse, rather than better. By the time we ended our conversation, the parents decided to keep their child in his local school and supplement his education with some additional hours of one-to-one therapy.

The articles in this section shed light on the different thinking and learning patterns of children with ASD. They offer many teaching tips to help children succeed. Among the different topics covered are areas that I view as especially important: developing the child's strengths, using a child's obsessions to motivate schoolwork, and teaching the child problem-solving and thinking skills that will assist him not just during his limited years in school, but throughout his entire life.

## BOOKS THAT GIVE INSIGHT INTO AUTISTIC THINKING AND LEARNING PATTERNS

Grandin, T. (2005). *Unwritten Rules of Social Relationships: Decoding Social Mysteries Through the Unique Perspectives of Autism.* Arlington, TX: Future Horizons, Inc.

Grandin T. (2006). *Thinking in Pictures* (Expanded Edition). New York: Vintage Press/Random House.

Tammet D. (2007). *Born on a Blue Day: Inside the Extraordinary Mind of an Autistic Savant.* New York: Free Press.

Most individuals on the spectrum have areas of strength that can be nurtured and developed into marketable employment skills.

# Finding a Child's
# Area of Strength

I N ONE OF MY 2005 COLUMNS IN THE AUTISM ASPERGER'S DIGEST, I
discussed the three different types of specialized thinking in individuals with high functioning autism and Asperger's Syndrome (HFA/AS). Children on the spectrum usually have an area of strength and an area of deficit. Many parents and teachers have asked me, "How do you determine the child's area of strength?" A child usually has to be at least in elementary school before it becomes evident. In many cases, the area of strength cannot be determined in a child younger than five years old. In some cases the area of strength doesn't emerge until some of the other, more dominant sensory or behavioral issues have been remediated.

The first type is the visual thinkers, who think in photo-realistic pictures. I am in this category, and my mind works like Google Images. When I was in elementary school, my visual thinking skills were expressed in art and drawing. Children who are visual thinkers will usually produce many beautiful drawings by the time they are in third or fourth grade. In my career, I use my visual thinking skills to design livestock-handling facilities. Visual thinkers often go into such careers as graphic arts, industrial design, or architecture.

The second type is the pattern thinkers, who are often very good at math and music. They see relationships and patterns between numbers and sounds. In elementary school, some of these children will play a musical instrument really well. Others will be good at both music and math, and another group will be math lovers with no musical interest. It is important to challenge these kids with advanced math. If they are forced to do "baby" math, they will get bored. If an elementary school student can do high school math, he or she should be encouraged to study it. Both photo-realistic visual thinkers and pattern thinkers often excel at building structures with blocks and Legos®. Pattern thinkers can have successful careers as engineers, computer programmers or musicians. However, the pattern thinkers will often need some extra help with reading and writing composition.

The third type is the verbal thinker. These children are word specialists and they know all the facts about their favorite subjects. For many of these kids, history is their favorite subject and their writing skills are good. The word thinkers are not visual thinkers and they will usually have little interest in art, drawing, or Legos. Individuals who are word specialists are often really good at journalism, being speech therapists, and any job that requires careful record keeping.

## Build Up Strengths

Too often educators pound away at the deficits and neglect to build up the child's area of strength. Most visual thinkers and some pattern thinkers cannot do algebra. Algebra was impossible for me, and therefore, I was never allowed to try geometry or trigonometry. Endless hours of algebra drills were useless. I did not understand it because there was nothing to visualize. When I discuss this at conferences, I find many children and adults on the spectrum who failed algebra, but were able to do geometry and trigonometry. They should be allowed to substitute these higher maths for algebra. Algebra is NOT the prerequisite for geometry and trigonometry for some types of brains. Educators need to understand that these individuals think differently and that what works for the typical-minded student may not work for the spectrum individual. I got through college math because in the

'60s, algebra had been replaced with finite math, where I studied probability and matrices. It was difficult but with tutoring I was able to do it. Finite math had things I could visualize. If I had been forced to take college algebra, I would have failed college math. Students should be allowed to substitute any higher math for algebra. One mother told me her son got straight As in college physics but he could not graduate from high school because he failed algebra.

In conclusion, focusing only on the deficits of individuals with HFA/AS does nothing to prepare them for the real world that lies outside of school. Most individuals on the spectrum have areas of strength that can be nurtured and developed into marketable employment skills. Teachers and parents need to build on these areas of strength starting when the child is young, and continue through middle and high school. In so doing, we provide these individuals with the opportunity to have satisfying careers they can enjoy for the rest of their lives.

Teachers and parents need
to help both children and adults
with autism take all the little details
they have in their head and put them
into categories to form concepts
and promote generalization.

# Teaching How to Generalize

MANY CHILDREN AND PEOPLE WITH AUTISM ARE NOT ABLE TO TAKE all the facts they know and link them together to form concepts. What has worked for me is to use my visual thinking to form concepts and categories. Explaining how I do this may help parents and professionals teach children with autism how to form concepts and generalizations.

When I was a little child, I knew that cats and dogs were different because dogs were bigger than cats. When the neighbors bought a little Dachshund, I could no longer categorize dogs by size. Rosie the Dachshund was the same size as a cat. I can remember looking intently at Rosie to find some visual characteristic that both our Golden Retriever and Rosie had in common. I noticed that all dogs, regardless of size, had the same kind of nose. Therefore, dogs could be placed in a separate category from cats because there are certain physical features that every dog has that no cat has.

Categorizing things can be taught. Little kindergarten children learn to categories all the red objects or all the square objects. Irene Pepperberg, a scientist at the University of Arizona, taught her parrot, Alex, to differentiate and identify objects by color and shape. He could pick out all the red square blocks from a tray containing red balls, blue square blocks, and red blocks. He understood categorization of objects by color, shape, and size. Teaching children and adults with autism to categorize and form concepts starts first with teaching simple categories such as color and shape. From this, we can help them understand that certain facts they have memorized can be placed in one category and other facts can be placed in another category.

## Teaching Concepts Such as Danger

Many parents have asked me, "How do I teach my child not to run into the street?" or "He knows not to run into the street at our house, but at Grandma's he runs into the street." In the first situation, the child actually has no concept of danger at all; in the second, he is not able to generalize what he has learned at home to a new house and street.

Danger as a concept is too abstract for the mind of a person who thinks in pictures. I did not understand that being hit by a car would be dangerous until I saw a squashed squirrel in the road and my nanny told me that it had been run over by a car. Unlike the cartoon characters on TV, the squirrel did not survive. I then understood the cause and effect of being run over.

After the squirrel incident, how did I learn that all cars on all streets are dangerous? It is just like learning concepts like the color red or square versus round. I had to learn that no matter where I was located, all cars and all streets had certain common features. When I was a child, safety concepts were drilled into my head with a book of safety songs. I sang about always looking both ways before crossing a street to make sure a car was not coming. To help me generalize, my nanny took my sister and me for walks around the neighborhood. On many different streets she had me look both ways before crossing. This is the same way that guide dogs for the blind are trained. The dog must be able to recognize stop lights, intersections, and streets in a strange place. During training, he is taken to many different streets. He then has visual, auditory and olfactory (smell) memories of many different streets. From these memories, the dog is able to recognize a street in a strange place.

For either the guide dog or the person with autism to understand the concept of *street*, they have to see more than one street. Autistic thinking is specific to general. To learn a concept of *dog* or *street*, I had to see many specific dogs or streets before the general concept could be formed. A general concept such as *street* without pictures of many specific streets stored in my memory bank is absolutely meaningless.

Autistic thinking is always detailed and specific. Teachers and parents need to help both children and adults with autism take all the little details they have in their head and put them into categories to form concepts and promote generalization.

Interests and talents
can turn into careers.

# The Importance
# of Developing Talent

THERE IS OFTEN TOO MUCH EMPHASIS IN THE WORLD OF AUTISM on the deficits of these children and not enough emphasis on developing the special talents that many of them possess. Talents need to be developed because they can form the basis of skills that will make a person with autism or Asperger's employable. Abilities such as drawing or math skills need to be nurtured and expanded. If a child likes to draw trains, that interest should be broadened into other activities, such as reading a book about trains or doing a math problem calculating the time it would take to travel from Boston to Chicago.

It is a mistake to stamp out a child's special interests, however odd they may seem at the time. In my own case, my talent in art was encouraged. My mother bought me professional art materials and a book on perspective drawing when I was in grade school.

Fixations and special interests should be directed into constructive channels instead of being abolished to make a person more "normal." The career I have today as a designer of livestock facilities is based on my talent areas. I use my visual thinking to design equipment. As a teenager, I became fixated on cattle squeeze chutes after I discovered that when I got in a cattle squeeze chute it relieved my anxiety. Fixations can be great motivators if they are properly channeled. My high school teacher directed my interest in cattle chutes into motivating me to study science and to study more in school. He told me that if I learned more about the field of sensory perception, I could find out why the pressure applied by the cattle chute was relaxing. Now, instead of boring everybody I knew with endless talk about cattle chutes, I immersed myself in the study of science. My original interest in the cattle chute also led to an interest in the behavior of cattle, then the design of systems, which led to the development of my career.

This is an example of taking a fixation and broadening it out into something constructive. Sometimes teachers and parents put so much emphasis on making a teenager more social that developing talents is neglected. Teaching social skills is very important, but if the person with autism is stripped of all their special interests, they may lose meaning in their life. "I am what I think and do, more than what I feel." Social interactions can be developed through shared interests. I had friends as a child because other children liked making craft projects with me. During the difficult years of high school, special interest clubs can be a lifesaver.

Recently I watched a TV documentary about autism. One of the people profiled liked to raise chickens. Her life took on meaning when she discovered that other people shared the same hobby. When she joined a poultry hobby club, she received social recognition for being an expert.

Interests and talents can turn into careers. Developing and nurturing these unique abilities can make life more fulfilling for a person with autism.

# Teaching People with Autism/Asperger's to Be More Flexible

RIGIDITY IN BOTH BEHAVIOR AND THINKING IS A MAJOR CHARACteristic of people with autism and Asperger's. They have difficulty understanding the concept that sometimes it is okay to break a rule. I heard about a case where an autistic boy had a severe injury but he did not leave the school bus stop to get help. He had been taught to stay at the bus stop so that he would not miss the bus; he could not break that rule. Common sense would have told most people that getting help for a severe injury would be more important than missing the bus. But not to this young man.

How can common sense be taught? I think it starts with teaching flexible thinking at a young age. Structure is good for children with autism, but sometimes plans can, and need to be, changed. When I was little, my nanny made my sister and me do a variety of activities. This variety prevented rigid behavior patterns from forming. I became more accustomed to changes in our daily or weekly routines and learned that I could still manage when change occurred. This same principle applies to animals. Cattle that are always fed from the red truck by Jim may panic if Sally pulls up in a white truck to feed them. To prevent this problem, progressive ranchers have learned to alter routines slightly so that cattle learn to accept some variation.

Another way to teach flexible thinking is to use visual metaphors, such as mixing paint. To understand complex situations, such as when occasionally a good friend does something nasty, I imagine mixing white and black paint. If the friend's behavior is mostly nice, the mixture is a very light gray; if the person is really not a friend then the mixture is a very dark gray.

Flexibility can also be taught by showing the person with autism that categories can change. Objects can be sorted by color, function, or material. To test this idea, I grabbed a bunch of black, red, and yellow objects in my office and laid them on the floor. They were a stapler, a roll of tape, a ball, videotapes, a toolbox, a hat, and pens. Depending upon the situation, any of these objects could be used for either work or play. Ask the child to give concrete examples of using a stapler for work or play. For instance, stapling office papers is work; stapling a kite together is play. Simple situations like this that teach a child flexibility in thinking and relating can be found numerous times in each day.

Children do need to be taught that some rules apply everywhere and should not be broken. To teach an autistic child to not run across the street, he has to be taught the rule in many different places; the rule has to be generalized and part of that process is making sure the child understands that the rule should not be broken. However, there are times when an absolute adherence to the rule can cause harm. Children also need to be taught that some rules can change depending on the situation. Emergencies are one such category where rules may be allowed to be broken.

Parents, teachers, and therapists can continually teach and reinforce flexible thinking patterns in children with autism/AS. I hope I have provided some ideas on how to do this while still accommodating the visual manner in which they think.

# Teaching Concepts to Children with Autism

G ENERALLY, PEOPLE WITH AUTISM POSSESS GOOD SKILLS IN LEARN-
ing rules, but they can have less developed abstract thinking
skills. Dr. Nancy Minshew and her colleagues at the University of
Pittsburgh have done research that may help teachers understand how
the autistic mind thinks. For the autistic, learning rules is easy, but
learning flexibility in thinking is difficult, and must be taught.

There are three basic levels of conceptual thinking: 1) learning rules,
2) identifying categories, and 3) inventing new categories. Category-
forming ability can be tested by placing a series of objects on a table,
such as pencils, notepads, cups, nail files, paper clips, napkins, bottles,
videotapes, and other common objects. A person with autism can easily identify all the pencils, or all the bottles. He can also easily identify
objects in simple categories, such as all the objects that are green or all
the metal objects. Conceptual thinking at this basic level is generally
not a problem.

Where the person with autism has extreme difficulty is inventing
new categories, which is the beginning of true concept formation. For
example, many of the objects in the list referenced above could be clas-
sified by use (i.e., office supplies) or by shape (round/not round). To
me, it is obvious that a cup, a bottle, and a pencil are all round. Most
people would classify a video cassette as not-round; however, I might
put it into the round category because of its round spools inside.

One of the easiest ways to teach concept formation is through playing category-forming games with children. For example, a cup can be used to drink from, or to store pencils or paper clips. In one situation, it is used for drinking; in the other, it is used in the office or at work. A videotape can be used for recreation or education, depending on the content of the tape. Notepads can be used for note taking, for art drawings, or, more abstractly, as a paperweight or a coaster for a glass. Activities such as these must be done with a high degree of repetition; it will take some time for the person with autism to learn to think differently. However, with perseverance, results will occur.

Helping children "get into their head" different and varied ways of categorizing objects is the first step in developing flexible thinking. The more examples provided, the more flexible his or her thinking can become. The more flexible the thinking, the easier it will be for the person with autism to learn to develop new categories and concepts. Once the child has acquired some flexible thinking skills with concrete objects, teachers can begin to expand their conceptual thinking into the less concrete areas of categorizing feelings, emotions, facial expressions, etc.

Flexible thinking is a highly important ability that is often—to the detriment of the child—omitted as a teachable skill on a child's IEP. It impacts a child in all environments, both now and in the future: school, home, relationships, employment, recreation. Parents and teachers need to give it more attention when developing a child's educational plan.

## REFERENCE

Minshew, N.J., J. Meyer, and G. Goldstein. 2002. Abstract reasoning in autism: A dissociation between concept formation and concept identification. *Neurospychology* 16: 327-334.

# Bottom-Up Thinking and Learning Rules

INDIVIDUALS ON THE AUTISM SPECTRUM LEARN TO FORM CONCEPTS by grouping many specific examples of a particular concept into a virtual "file folder" in their brain. There may be a file folder labeled "Dogs," full of many mental pictures of different kinds of dogs—together, all those mental pictures form a concept of "Dog." A person on the autism spectrum may have many of these virtual file folders in their brain—one for each different concept (rudeness, turn-taking, street safety, etc.). As a person grows older, they create new file folders and add new pictures to the ones in their old file folders.

People on the autism spectrum think differently from non-autistic, or "typical" people. They are "bottom-up," or "specific-to-general" thinkers. For example, they may need to see many, many different kinds of dogs before the concept of dog is permanently fixed in their mind. Or they may need to be told many times, in many places, that they must stop, look, and listen before crossing the street before the concept of street safety is permanently fixed in their mind. People on the spectrum create the concepts of dog, street safety, and everything else by "building" them from many specific examples.

Non-autistic, or "typical" people think in a completely different way. They are "top-down thinkers," or "general-to-specific" thinkers. They form a concept first, and then add in specific details. For example, they already have a general concept of what a dog looks like, and as they see more and more dogs, they add the details of what all kinds of different dogs (poodles, basset hounds, dachshunds, etc.) look like. Once someone tells them to stop, look, and listen before crossing the street, they know to do this at every street, in every neighborhood.

Bottom-up learning can be used to teach both very concrete and more abstract concepts ranging from basic safety rules to reading comprehension. In this article I will give examples starting from the most concrete concepts and finishing with more abstract ones. All concepts, regardless of the level of abstraction, *must* be taught with many *specific examples* for each concept.

To teach a basic safety rule, such as not running across the street, it must be taught in more than one place. This is required to make the safety rule "generalize" to new places. It must be taught at the street at home, at streets near the school, at the next-door neighbor's house, at streets around grandmother's house, or Aunt Georgia's house, and when the child visits a new, strange place. The number of different specific examples required will vary from child to child. When I was little, I was taught turn-taking with a board game called Parcheesi. If my turn-taking lessons had been limited to this game they would not have generalized to other situations, such as taking turns with my sister to use a sled or a toy. During all of these activities, I was told I had to take turns. Turn-taking in conversation was also taught at the dining room table. If I talked too long, mother told me I had to give someone else a turn to talk.

Using many specific examples should also be used for teaching number concepts. To achieve generalization, a child should be taught counting, adding, and subtracting, with many different kinds of objects. You can use cups, candies, toy dinosaurs, pens, Matchbook cars, and other things to teach the abstract idea that arithmetic applies to many things in the real world. For example $5 - 2 = 3$ can be taught with five candies. If I eat 2 of them, I have 3 left. To learn concepts such as less and more, or fractions, try using cups of water filled to different levels, cutting up an apple, and cutting up cardboard circles. If you only used cardboard circles, the child might think that the concept of fractions applies only to cardboard circles. To teach bigger versus smaller, use different-sized objects such as bottles, candies, shirts, blocks, toy cars, and other things.

## More Abstract Concepts

To move up a degree in the abstractness of concepts, I will give some examples for teaching concepts such as "up" and "down." Again, you must use many specific examples to teach these concepts.

The squirrel is "up" in the tree.
The stars are "up" in the sky.
We throw the ball "up" in the air.

We slide "down" the slide.
We dig a hole "down" in the ground.
We bend "down" to tie our shoes.

To fully comprehend the concept, the child needs to participate in the activity while the parent or teacher says a short sentence containing the word "up" or "down." Be sure to vocally emphasize the concept word. If the child has difficulty with verbal language, combine the word with a picture card that says "up" or "down."

Recently I was asked, "How did you comprehend the concept of rude behavior or good table manners?" Concepts that relate to judgments or social expectations are much more abstract for a child, yet they can still be taught in the same way. When I did something that was bad table manners, such as waving my fork in the air, mother explained to me—very simply and without a lot of verbal chatter—that it was bad table manners. "Temple, waving your fork in the air is bad table manners." She used many naturally occurring teachable moments, helping me connect my action to the concept "bad table manners." She did this matter-of-factly and kept the message simple and consistent. Learning many specific examples also worked when she taught me the concept of rudeness. When I did something that was rude, such as belching or cutting in line, mother told me I was being rude. Gradually a "rude" concept formed in my brain from the many specific examples.

## Reading Comprehension

Many children on the spectrum can decode and read, but they have problems with comprehension. To start, focus on the very concrete facts, such as characters' names, cities they visited, or activities they did, such as playing golf. This is generally easier for the child to comprehend. Then move on to more abstract concepts in a passage of literature. For example, if they read, "Jim ate eggs and bacon" they may have difficulty answering the multiple-choice question: "Did Jim eat breakfast, lunch, or dinner?" Teach the child to break apart the question and scan his or her brain files for information that may help with comprehension. For instance, I would search through the files in my brain for pictures of meals. A picture of eggs with bacon is the best match for breakfast compared to lunch and dinner pictures.

These more abstract concepts and associations don't develop quickly. The child will need to add more and more information into his brain computer before he can be successful with abstractions. This data comes from experiences, which is why parents and teachers need to give the child lots and lots of opportunities for repetitive practice on a concept or lesson. I would start to learn this sort of concept only after a teacher had explained many different stories to me.

# Motivating
# Students

ONE FREQUENT CHARACTERISTIC OF INDIVIDUALS ON THE AUTISM/
Asperger's spectrum is an obsessive interest in one or a few particular subjects, to the exclusion of others. These individuals may be near-genius on a topic of interest, even at a very early age. Parents have described to me their ten-year-old child whose knowledge of electricity rivals that of a college senior, or a near-teen whose knowledge of insects far surpasses that of his biology teacher. However, as motivated as they are to study what they enjoy, these students are often equally unmotivated when it comes to schoolwork outside their area of interest.

It was like this with me when I was in high school. I was totally unmotivated about schoolwork in general. But I was highly motivated to work on the things that interested me, such as showing horses, painting signs, and doing carpentry projects. Luckily, my mother and some of my teachers used my special interests to keep me motivated. Mr. Carlock, my science teacher, took my obsessive interests in cattle chutes and the squeeze machine to motivate me to study science. The squeeze machine relaxed me. Mr. Carlock told me that if I really wanted to know why the machine had this effect, I would have to study the boring school subjects so that I could graduate and then go to college to become a scientist who could answer this question. Once I really grasped the idea that to get from here to there—from middle school to graduation to college and then to a job of interest to me—I needed to apply myself to all my school subjects, boring or not. This understanding maintained my motivation to complete the work.

While students are in elementary school, teachers can easily keep them involved by using a special interest to motivate their learning. An example would be taking a student's interest in trains and using a train theme in many different subjects. In history class, read about the history of the railroad; in math class, involve trains in problem solving; in science class, discuss different forms of energy that trains utilized then and now, etc.

As students move into middle and high school, they can get turned on by visiting interesting work places, such as a construction site, an architecture firm, or a research lab. This makes the idea of a career real to the student and they begin to understand the education path they must take early on in school to achieve that career. If visiting a work site is not possible, invite parents who have interesting jobs into the school classroom to talk with students about their jobs. Lots of pictures to show what the work is like are strongly recommended. This is also an opportunity for students to hear about the social side of employment, which can provide motivation for making new friends, joining groups or venturing out into social situations that might be uncomfortable at first.

Students on the spectrum need to be exposed to new things in order to become interested in them. They need to see concrete examples of really cool things to keep them motivated to learn. I became fascinated by optical illusions after seeing a single movie in science class that demonstrated optical illusions. My science teacher challenged me to recreate two famous optical illusions, called the Ames Distorted Room and the Ames Trapezoidal Window. I spent six months making them out of cardboard and plywood and I finally figured them out. This motivated me to study experimental psychology in college.

## Bring Trade Magazines to the Library

Scientific journals, trade magazines, and business newspapers can show students a wide range of careers and help turn students on to the opportunities available after they graduate. Every profession, from the most complex to the practical, has its trade journal. Trade magazines are published in fields as diverse as banking, baking, car wash operation, construction, building maintenance, electronics, and many others. Parents who already work in these fields could bring their old trade journals to the school library. These magazines would provide a window into the world of jobs and help motivate students.

## ADDITIONAL MATH, SCIENCE, AND GRAPHICS RESOURCES

About.com's Animation Channel – free animation software, plus free articles and tutorials. *Animation.about.com*

Foldit – an online game where students can solve protein-folding chemistry problems and make real contributions to medical science. (The more we know about how certain proteins fold, the better new proteins we can design to combat the disease-related proteins and cure the diseases.) *Fold.it*

Google Sketchup – free drawing/3D-modeling software. *Sketchup.google.com*

The National Science Digital Library – a national network of learning environments and resources for science, technology, engineering, and mathematics education at all levels. *Nsdl.org*

OpenCourseWare Consortium – free college course materials. *Ocwconsortium.org*

Physics Education Technology (PhET) – Fun, interactive, science simulations, from the PhET project at the University of Colorado. *Phet.colorado.edu*

Wolfram Alpha – a knowledge engine that doesn't find information, but instead computes information based on built-in data, algorithms, and methods. *Wolframalpha.com*

Wolfram MathWorld – a really awesome mathematics site that serves as a wiki encyclopedia of equations, theorems, algorithms, and more. *Mathworld.wolfram.com*

If my third grade teacher had
continued trying to teach me
to read with endless, boring drills,
I would have failed the
reading competency tests required
by No Child Left Behind.

# Getting Kids Turned On to Reading

ONE COMPLAINT I AM HEARING FROM BOTH PARENTS AND TEACHERS is that the No Child Left Behind law makes it impossible to spend much time on subjects other than reading and math because school districts put so much emphasis on students passing tests in these subjects. Recently, I had a discussion with a mom about teaching reading. She told me that her daughter, who has reading problems, was not allowed to go outside for recess because she had to do reading drills. The girl was bored stiff and hated it. However, she quickly learned to read when her mom taught her from a Harry Potter book. To motivate kids, especially those with autism spectrum disorders, you need to start with books the kids want to read. The Harry Potter series is one of the best things that has happened to reading instruction. Two hours before the last Harry Potter book went on sale, I visited the local Barnes and Noble. It was jammed full of kids in costume and a line stretched half way around the block. I think it is wonderful that the kids were getting so turned on about a book.

I could not read when I was in third grade. Mother taught me to read after school from an interesting book about Clara Barton, a famous nurse. The content kept me interested, and motivated me to learn, even though the book was written at the sixth grade level.

Mother taught me how to sound out the words, and within three months, my reading skills jumped two grade levels on standardized tests. I was a phonics learner, but other kids on the autism spectrum are visual, sight-word learners. When they read the word *dog*, they see a picture of a dog in their head. Children are different; parents should identify which way their child learns best and then use that method.

Sight-word readers usually learn nouns first. To learn the meaning of words like *went* and *going* I had to see them in a sentence I could visualize. For example, "I *went* to the supermarket" or "I am *going* to the supermarket." One is past and the other is future. When I *went* to the supermarket I see myself with the bag of groceries I purchased. When I say I am *going* to the supermarket, I see myself driving there. Use examples the child can visualize and relate to when teaching all the connector words that are not easily visualized themselves.

If my third grade teacher had continued trying to teach me to read with endless, boring drills, I would have failed the reading competency tests required by school systems that are "teaching to the test" to obtain better school-wide ranking on standardized tests. After mother taught me reading, I was able to do really well on the elementary school reading tests. She got me engaged in reading in a way that was meaningful to me until reading became naturally reinforcing on its own.

Parents and teachers can use a child's special interests or natural talents in creative ways to teach basic academic skills such as reading and math. Science and history make wonderfully interesting topics to teach both subjects to spectrum children. If the child likes dinosaurs, teach reading using books about dinosaurs. A simple math problem might be rewritten using dinosaurs as the subject or new exercises created by the adult. For example: if a dinosaur walks at five miles per hour, how far can he walk in fifteen minutes?

Students with ASD can get excellent scores on standardized tests when more creative methods are used that appeal to their interests and ways of thinking. Although this creative effort may take a little more time at the onset, the improved learning, interest and motivation in the child will more than make up for the extra time in the long run.

# Turning Video Game Obsessions into Learning

I'M A FIRM BELIEVER THAT THERE ARE CERTAIN CHARACTERISTICS OF autism and Asperger's that can be used to a person's advantage, if channeled in the right way by the parents and educators involved with the child. One of these characteristics is the obsessive interest children often have in things. Parents ask me all the time: how do I help my child become interested in learning when all he wants to do is play video games or draw Japanese anime cartoons? My response is this: turn that video game obsession into learning opportunities!

Often the most effective method is to use elements of the game or the cartoons that can be applied to other activities. Many popular games are based on a quest for a goal. Inspire a child to read by explaining that there exist great works of literature about quests that have similarities to those in a video game. King Arthur and his knights of the Round Table were on a quest. Another example might be taking a child's Superman fixation and using it to motivate learning in math and science. For example, how long would it take Superman to fly across the U.S. at the speed of sound?

The Mario video games center around a character who is a plumber. This could be used in a way to start an interest in plumbing or to practice problem-solving skills. You could ask the child, "What does Mario do when he is not in the video game? He fixes pipes." Or ask the child to connect different sizes and shapes of pipe to get from location A to

B, or use different plumbing supplies as sorting objects, or to hone math skills.

If a child spends hours drawing the same cartoon over and over again, use that obsession as the starting point to broaden the subject matter of the drawings. Instead of endless pictures of Mickey Mouse, you might suggest drawing Mickey's house, or Mickey's car. To channel the huge motivation the fixation provides into a new direction, there must be a direct association between the existing fixation and the new request. As the child's mind becomes more flexible, you can broaden the associations into other areas that address new skills. For instance, after drawing Mickey's house, suggest drawing Mickey eating dinner, then Mickey setting the table or Mickey helping Mom prepare dinner.

For some children, video games border on obsessions because of the visual stimulation they hold. If video games had been available when I was growing up, I would have been addicted to them if I had been allowed to play them all day; I loved watching rapid movement. (Mother would never have permitted that.) While there are some children who have the skills to become successful video game programmers, I am not one of them. The games would have been a distraction from learning other skills I needed. In my case, I would have spent my time playing video games instead of developing my talent for building things. I might have ended up unemployable instead of becoming as successful as I am today.

The way I see it, video game playing should be limited to an hour per day, or some other finite amount of time that is reasonable for the individual. If left unchecked, true obsessions can prevent a child from engaging in other activities that will benefit his learning and development in the long run. Parents need to step in and be firm in curbing obsessions by transforming them into more productive activities in the child's life. This may be difficult at first, with much resistance on the part of the child—especially if he has been allowed free rein in his obsessions for months or years. He may not understand why it was okay to play these games as much as he wanted before and now it is no longer so. Parents must be patient and creative in how they approach this situation, and gradually reduce the time spent on video games while stimulating interest in other activities by using the game components as the bridge between the two.

Remember a basic principle in working with autistic individuals: an obsession or fixation has huge motivation potential for the child. Video games are one such fixation shared by many individuals on the spectrum. He will work at learning new things or new activities to gain access to his video games. Use that to your advantage to help him grow and expand his understanding of the world beyond that of hand-held games.

Parents, are you willing and
able to make the time, financial,
and emotional commitment
of having a service dog?